Cambridge Primary

Revise for Cambridge Primary Checkpoint

English
Study Guide

Stephanie Austwick

Series editor: Kate Ruttle

HODDER
EDUCATION
AN HACHETTE UK COMPANY

Contents

Sentence structure and punctuation

Phonics and spelling

Glossary

About this Study Guide

It is a well-known fact that if you want to be good at something, you have to practise!

This **Study Guide** will help you practise and revise all the English skills you have been taught ready for the Cambridge Primary Checkpoint English tests.

It is organised into four chapters – Reading genres; Writing skills; Sentence structure and punctuation; and Phonics and spelling.

Each chapter contains key facts, texts, examples and activities. Working through these will help to improve your English skills.

> **Key facts** This section appears at the start of each double page and acts as a reminder of useful information. Reading this will help you to remember lots of important things to improve your reading and writing skills. Sometimes it includes model texts to help with writing or developing **comprehension** skills. Glossary words are shown in bold in the Key facts section. See pages 94–95 for the Glossary.

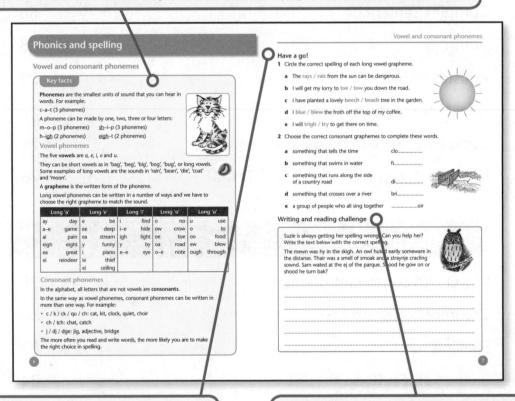

> **Have a go!** This section gives you a chance to practise some of your English skills. There is a wide variety of activities on offer, which cover all the main points.

> **Reading** and / or **Writing challenge** This section includes further ideas for you to explore. They may involve doing some research, writing for fun or making a game.

How much can you remember? Tests

Using this section at the end of each chapter, see what you can remember about all the things you have been taught. When the tests have been marked, it is a good idea to check up on any mistakes. That way, you won't make them again.

Completing activities

ALWAYS read the information and the questions thoroughly!

Wherever you see this image of a sheet of paper, answer the questions in a separate exercise book:

Take time to complete the activities to the very best of your ability and try to follow these four basic rules:

1 Rehearse what you are going to write in your head before you put it down on paper.

2 Re-read what you have written to check that it makes sense and that spelling and punctuation are accurate.

3 Make changes to improve your work where necessary. These might be word choices, sentence structures or information.

4 Always present your work clearly, taking care with your handwriting.

Tips for revision

Vision means 'to see'. Therefore *re-vision* means 'to see again' or 'to revisit something'. We are taught a great deal as we go through life and it is quite hard to keep all this information in our heads. Therefore, it is really helpful to remind ourselves now and again, and the more times we remind ourselves, the easier things become.

Here are some simple ways to improve your literacy knowledge and develop valuable skills for life:

• Use this book as a revision guide to revisit things you have been taught. Read the information, enjoy the texts, have a go at the activities and explore the challenges. Talk about them with your friends. Little and often is the key – revisit a little bit at a time, but come back to it again and again. You will find that this is the best way to become an expert in English.

• Whether you are a fan of fiction or non-fiction, by reading a range of text types you will be revising without even knowing it! Reading is not only an enjoyable pastime, it also expands your general knowledge, develops your powers of comprehension, increases your vocabulary, helps you with spelling, reminds you of sentence and text structures and provides you with models for your own writing. Wow! It's worth doing!

Make the most of other resources

If you are lucky enough to have access to technology, make the most of computers for research or to present your work. On a less technical level, take time to use a dictionary to check and improve your spelling, or a thesaurus to expand your knowledge of words and provide you with choices for the future.

Good luck!

Reading genres

Historical stories – settings

Historical stories are set at a time in the past. They often include:

- unfamiliar vocabulary
- old-fashioned ideas and **phrases**.

When reading these texts, it is important to look out for details that tell you about the time when the story takes place. Comparing the **setting**, **characters** and actions with your own experiences today can tell you a lot about how things have changed since historical times.

Model text

There was once a merchant and his wife, who lived in Holland many centuries ago. This was the time when tulip bulbs were terribly valuable, because everyone wanted to see different kinds of tulips: plain colours, patterned colours, stripes and fluted petals. The best tulips used to raise thousands of guilders!

This merchant was especially good at growing tulips. He was breeding the bulbs, and developing the best colour combinations in the whole of Holland. He kept them in the dark under the stairs, but occasionally brought them out when he was ready to put them in for prizes. And this was what he did one winter's evening, when he was getting ready for the biggest awards of the year.

That evening the merchant's wife was in a hurry to prepare dinner, as she was going out to lace-making classes. So she didn't even bother to light the oil lamp on the wall in the kitchen, but just chopped up all the ingredients for a stew and put them into the pot that was hanging over the fire in the hearth.

Just imagine what the merchant felt when he went into the kitchen after his wife had gone out, and searched for the prize bulb he'd put out ready. Just imagine his language when he found the onion peelings in the pail by the door. No, they weren't onion peelings, they were the skin of his prize tulip bulb, skulking at the bottom of the pail with all the leftovers from dinner …

merchant – someone who buys and sells goods for a living

tulip – a colourful flower

bulb – a fleshy underground stem that stores food for the shoot within

guilders – currency used in Holland before 2002

hearth – the area around the fireplace

pail – a bucket

Have a go!

Read the historical story on the opposite page and answer these questions:

1 When and where is this story set?

....

2 Why was the merchant trying to 'breed' the best tulips?

....

3 Write down two things from paragraph 3 that make you think it might not be a modern story.

....

....

4 What had happened to the prize tulip bulb and why?

....

....

5 How do you think the merchant felt when he realised what had happened?

....

....

Writing challenge 📄

Imagine you are the merchant's wife and, later that evening, you write up a diary of the day's events. Describe what happened in the story, as if you had been there. Remember that it is a historical story.

You could start:
A terrible thing happened today. I had been so busy and …

Fantasy stories – characters

Key facts

Fantasy stories are a product of the imagination. They often include:

- unusual or magical settings, such as other worlds
- strange **characters**, such as made-up creatures or animals that can talk
- impossible or improbable actions and outcomes, such as time travel.

Model text

Rebecca pointed a shaking finger. 'Look!'

Deep inside the bushes was a single yellow eye that stared unblinkingly at them. A few yards to the right another eye appeared, gleaming like a headlight of a motor-bike. Yet another eye glinted off to their left.

'Swardlewardles!' gulped Grisby.

The bushes quaked and shook as the creatures, seemingly oblivious to the sharp thorns, pushed their way towards the frightened group.

The first of the Swardlewardles waddled out of the bushes, leaving behind it a narrow tunnel that marked its path. Its companions crunched into the open and stood, glaring maliciously.

They were strange-looking creatures. The single eye was situated in the centre of a broad forehead. Below it was a nose or snout that contained three nostrils, and below that was a mouth that had so many teeth it resembled the keyboard of a piano. The bulky body and the long tail were covered with gleaming silver scales, hard and metallic looking. It was this armour-plating that protected them from the thorns.

A dozen more Swardlewardles had now emerged. They stood in a loose circle surrounding the friends. The largest of them shuffled forward. It only had short legs, but there were hundreds of them. It opened its mouth and gave a sinister, gurgling roar. A cloud of bluey white smoke belched from its trio of nostrils.

Have a go!

Read the passage on the opposite page and answer these questions.

1 How do you know this is a fantasy story?

....

2 How do you think Rebecca is feeling at the start of the passage and what makes you think this?

....

....

3 Find the **simile** the author uses to describe the single yellow eye.

....

4 Find the word 'oblivious' in the passage. What does it mean?

....

....

5 There is also a simile describing the mouth of the Swardlewardle but it doesn't use the word 'as' or 'like'. Write down the complete simile.

....

....

Reading challenge

Read the passage again very carefully, underlining or highlighting all the descriptions of the Swardlewardles.

1 Draw your impression of what a Swardlewardle might look like.

2 Compare it with a friend's drawing.

3 Discuss:

  • the importance of giving clear descriptions of the characters in stories, allowing readers to picture them in their minds

  • the power of similes – how do they help the reader?

9

Stories from other cultures – inference and atmosphere

Key facts

People tell and write stories all over the world. Stories from other cultures:

- show us how other people live – their traditions, lifestyles and homes
- include people, places, beliefs and activities that are familiar to those cultures
- use some words from the local language.

Model text

During the morning mist, the fog swirled up around Mat, Martha and their daddy. And when they sat cross-legged, they couldn't be seen from afar. But they were there.

Then Daddy Wes told them a story in his soft voice, the voice that could tap, tap, tap Mat and Martha very gently on their hearts.

Daddy Wes began.

'Long before time, before hours and minutes and seconds, on the continent of Africa, the rhythm of the Earth beat for the first people.

The Earth filled the air with spirit.

The spirit rose on the wind and flew into our bodies. And our own hearts beat for the first time. We were alive!

The beat moved through our bodies and pushed out from our fingers. This is how our drum was born.

With the drum we spoke to the animals and to the people.

The Earth's heart beat out the rhythm of all there is. We listened – and sounded the rhythms back for her to hear.

Then men from another continent came – men who would not listen to the rhythm of the Earth.

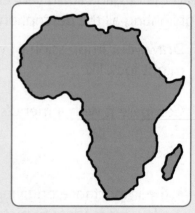

They shackled us, the people of the Earth's colour, and flung us into the bellies of ships, bringing us enslaved across the oceans and the seas.

They tore us apart from one another and did not allow us to speak our own languages. We were a lost people. We were no longer free. We thought we were no more.

Then they took our drums away.'

Have a go!

Read the passage on the opposite page and answer these questions.

1 Who was Daddy Wes telling the story to?

....

2 What do you think the author means by 'his soft voice, the voice that could tap, tap, tap Mat and Martha very gently on their hearts'?

....

....

3 Why do you think Daddy Wes told stories like this?

....

....

....

4 The beating of the drum is a **metaphor** for life and living – for being 'at one' with the Earth and with the beauty of Africa. Who didn't listen to the rhythm of the drum?

....

5 The mood at the beginning of the story is peaceful and calm. What is the mood in the last part of the story?

....

....

6 Find an example of a word, phrase or sentence that you think is particularly effective in creating a mood or atmosphere. Explain your choice.

....

....

....

Reading challenge

Read some other stories that reflect different cultures. Think about how the author creates atmosphere and mood in these examples.

Stories with issues – authors and viewpoints

Key facts

Stories with issues may:

- cover difficult subjects – for example: conservation, bullying, death
- make readers think about difficult questions
- put across a point of view.

When reading these stories, it is important to consider the **viewpoint** from which a story is written. Authors sometimes express their own viewpoint or write as if the reader is looking through the eyes of a narrator. The narrator is often one of the main **characters**.

Model text

Here is a page from a book that Lauren Child wrote and illustrated – *Utterly Me, Clarice Bean.*

When I get downstairs, the whole kitchen is full of a bad mood. Marcie won't talk to Mum, and Kurt won't talk to Marcie. Grandad isn't talking to anyone because he hasn't plugged himself into his hearing-aid. Minal is talking to me but I wish he wouldn't. Minal is a niggling gnat and I have to have him sleeping in my room. Sometimes, when I want to keep him out, I pile lots of gubbins against the door. He is five. Who wants to share a room with a five-year-old brother? I don't even need a five-year-old brother. I already have one who is a teenager called Kurt and that is enough brothers for anyone.

Have a go!

Read the passage on the opposite page and answer these questions.

1 How many people are there in the kitchen? ....

2 How many people are talking? ....

3 Which tense is the story written in and why?

....

4 From whose viewpoint is the story being told?

....

5 What is her opinion of her brothers?

....

6 What do you think 'gubbins' means?

....

7 Why does the author use the question, 'Who wants to share a room with a five-year-old brother?' What effect does this have on the reader?

....

....

8 What issues might this story be dealing with? Try to think of three.

   a ....

   b ....

   c ....

Writing challenge 📄

Clarice is now in the kitchen with her family. What happens next? Write the next paragraph from her point of view.

Fables, myths and legends – the parts of a story

Key facts

Fables, myths and legends are all traditional stories, often handed down from generation to generation. Each type of story has special features:

Fable – short story; untrue; often involves animals; teaches a moral at the end

Myth – can be a longer story; often includes monsters, gods, heroes and villains, talking animals, and so on; untrue; can sometimes be used to explain a wonder of nature

Legend – can be a longer story; may not be true but is often based on truth, such as a real person, place or event that people have added to over time.

Model text

There was once a lioness and her cubs. The first cub was boisterous, and often fell into streams and ditches. The second cub was always careful and obedient, and rather boring. The third cub was so shy that he never let go of his mother's tail.

One day they went off hunting in the bush, hoping to catch a small deer.

'There's one,' said the lioness. 'See if you can catch it!'

The first cub gave a great whoop and leaped so high that he fell into the river, and frightened the small deer away.

The third cub started wailing, and hid behind a large cactus.

The second cub waited patiently and then tracked down the deer so that they could all eat supper.

Moral: Look before you leap. (But life would be boring if we were all the same!)

Have a go!

Read the story above and answer these questions.

1 Do you think this is a fable, a myth or a legend? Give reasons for your answer.

....

....

2 Who is the only character to use **direct speech**?

....

3 Why do you think the author gives each cub a different personality at the beginning?

....

....

4 There is one moral at the end of the story. Write down two alternative morals that the author could place at the end.

a ....

....

b ....

....

Reading and writing challenge 📄

1 Read some other fables, myths and legends from different parts of the world, for example Aesop's fables.

Look out for common themes, and similarities and differences.

Find out if there are any legends connected with people or places that are local to you.

2 Write your own fable with three contrasting characters. Use this plan to help you.

Original	Plan	Your version
Introduce lioness and three cubs – different personalities	Opening – introduce setting and characters – three personalities	
Go off hunting	Build-up – leading to a task	
First cub and third cub fail	Action – two fail, linked to personalities	
Second cub is successful	Resolution – one is successful	
Moral	Moral	

Poetry – figurative language

Key facts

There are many different types of poem:

- some poems are set out in verses and have clear rhythm and rhyme

- free verse does not have a clear rhythm or rhyme, but the poet carefully chooses the words for effect

- **narrative** poems tell a story and may be several verses long

- some poems are in the form of a list

- some types of poetry, such as haiku, have specific rules.

Authors and poets use a variety of language features, such as **similes**, **metaphors** and **alliteration**, to make their descriptions come to life. These often make it easier for readers to build up an image in their minds. We call this figurative language.

Model text   Willow and Ginkgo by Eve Merriam

The willow is like an etching,
Fine-lined against the sky.
The ginkgo is like a crude sketch,
Hardly worthy to be signed.
The willow's music is like a soprano,
Delicate and thin.
The ginkgo's tune is like a chorus
With everyone joining in.

The willow is sleek as a velvet-nosed calf;
The ginkgo is leathery as an old bull.
The willow's branches are like silken thread;
The ginkgo's like stubby rough wool.

The willow is like a nymph with streaming hair;
Wherever it grows, there is green and gold and fair.
The willow dips to the water,
Protected and precious, like the king's favourite daughter.

The gingko forces its way through grey concrete;
Like a city child, it grows up in the street.
Thrust against the metal sky,
Somehow it survives and even thrives.
My eyes feast upon the willow,
But my heart goes to the ginkgo.

Have a go!

Read the poem on the opposite page and answer these questions.

1 This poem is full of similes. Write down two similes used to describe the willow.

    a ....

       ....

    b ....

       ....

2 Write two similes used to describe the ginkgo.

    a ....

       ....

    b ....

       ....

3 Write down an example of alliteration the writer uses in the poem.

    ....

4 Why do you think the poet uses the description 'metal sky'?

    ....

5 In the last two lines, the poet says how she feels about the two trees. Explain her feelings in your own words, including some of the reasons she gives in the poem.

Reading and writing challenge

1 Read other examples of poems that use figurative language to describe a person, a place, an animal or an object.

2 Choose two contrasting places, animals or objects that you are familiar with, for example a snake and a bird, or the sun and the moon. Write a simile poem in the style of the poem opposite, comparing the two. Choose your words carefully to create an effective poem.

Playscripts

Key facts

A playwright is someone who writes playscripts.

The playwright creates the scene and develops the **characters** using the stage directions, and carefully chooses words for the characters to say (**dialogue**). An actor or director must then decide how to use both of these to make the story come to life.

Playscripts are set out in a very clear way, with the character's name on the left, the dialogue on the right and the stage directions in brackets or italics or both.

Model text

Scene 1:

Early morning. A dusty, deserted road. A young girl is waiting impatiently outside her friend's front door. She knocks. She seems flustered and is looking anxiously all around. She knocks again – louder this time.

Footsteps are heard inside.

Jamelia: (*from inside*) OK, OK! Keep your hair on. (*opening door*) Abbi! What on earth is the matter?

Abbi: (*grabbing Jamelia's arm and beginning to pull her outside*) You've got to come quickly.

Jamelia: (*resisting*) Hey! Hang on a moment. What's going on? Come where?

Abbi: To my house. Something terrible has happened. Come on. Quick!

Jamelia: (*shaking her arm free*) Wait. I'll have to tell Mum where I'm going.

Abbi: (*suddenly looking panic stricken*) No! Don't do that! Don't tell your mum – there isn't time. We have to go NOW! It might be too late.

(*She turns and begins to run down the path.*)

Jamelia: (*starting to follow*) Too late for what? What's going on? Is it your family? What's happened, Abbi?

Abbi: I'll explain on the way. Come on!

Both girls begin to run.

Have a go!

Read the play-script on the opposite page and answer these questions.

1 What is the setting for the opening of the play?

....

2 How many children are there?

....

3 How is Abbi feeling at the beginning? Give details from both the description and the words she says.

....

....

....

4 What does Jamelia want to do before she leaves?

....

5 List three features of playscripts.

   a ....

   b ....

   c ....

Reading and writing challenge

1 Read the extract aloud several times with a friend, but try saying the lines in different ways, to give the characters different personalities.

For example, Jamelia might be grumpy, or unfriendly or scared. Abbi might shout, or whisper. Think about how changes affect the characters and the situation.

2 A 'line' is the term given to what a character says, even though it might take up several 'lines' of writing. There are eight lines in the extract opposite.

Imagine Jamelia *does* go back into the house to speak to her mum before she leaves. Write eight lines of dialogue between Jamelia and her mum. Make sure you use all the features of a play-script and build the scene through the dialogue and stage directions.

Autobiographies

> ### Key facts
>
> An **autobiography** is a life story written by the subject of the story. It is a **recount** of events in the author's life. An autobiography is **non-fiction**, but some authors use an autobiographical style when writing **fiction**. This is when the text appears to have been written by the main **character**, recounting past events.

> ### Model text   Benita's diary
>
> Dear Diary
>
> Today I got a new go-cart. It is very exciting and I am quite sure I am going to be a star. Just as soon as I get it into working order. But let me explain …
>
> My brother Milton is very good with his hands. So, with that in mind, I took it upon myself to rescue the Hope Street Gang's old go-cart, which they'd unceremoniously dumped on the empty lot on the corner.
>
> When I looked at the go-cart I didn't see the missing wheels or the broken axle. I didn't see the ripped seat or the missing panels. I didn't even see the frayed and knotted steering rope. All I saw was a freshly painted speeding cart carrying me triumphantly to glory in the next local race.
>
> It was quite a mission to get the cart home. I think I may have noticed the lack of wheels at that stage, but I persevered, pushing and dragging it up the block. People looked at me like I was quite mad. I was too busy sweating and struggling to really take any notice.
>
> When I got the cart home, Milton wasn't there. My mum took one look at it, raised her one eyebrow and said, 'Why you drag dat ole wreck home? What you gone do wit it?'
>
> 'I'm going to race it,' I said, as if it was the most obvious thing in the world.
>
> 'Tchhh,' my mum said, turning around to go inside. 'Don you go be leavin that in my front yard. Neighbours gon tink we gon mad.'
>
> I just sighed. Clearly my mother could not see the potential that I saw in this magnificent racing machine.
>
>

Have a go!

Read the diary entry on the opposite page and answer these questions.

1 Where did Benita get her new go-cart?

....

2 Was it in good condition? How do you know?

....

....

3 How did Benita get it home?

....

4 Was her mother pleased to see it? How can you tell?

....

....

5 What do you notice about the way the text is written – for example, informal or formal style, first or third person, past or present tense?

....

....

Reading and writing challenge

1 Find other texts that are autobiographical.

Look out for any fiction texts that use an autobiographical style.

2 Write a short passage about a memory you have from when you were younger.

....

....

....

....

....

Biographies

Key facts

A **biography** is a life story of a person written by someone else.

This biography comes from the publisher's website for author Lauren Child, who wrote the *Clarice Bean* books.

Model text   Author information: Lauren Child

Lauren Child grew up in Wiltshire (in the UK) as the middle child of three sisters and the daughter of two teachers. She has always been interested in the many aspects of childhood, from gazing into toy shop windows to watching American children's shows from the 1960s.

After attending two art schools, where Lauren admits that she did not learn much, she travelled for six months, still unsure about which career to embark upon.

Before Lauren started writing and illustrating children's books she started her own company 'Chandeliers for the People', making exotic, elegant lampshades. It was only when she came to write and illustrate the book *Clarice Bean, That's Me* that she decided to devote her time to writing and illustrating books for children, which combines her fascination for childhood and her talent for designing and creating.

Lauren gets her inspiration from other people's conversations or from seeing something funny happen.

This is an example of Lauren Child's illustrations, taken from the book *Clarice Bean, That's Me.* See pages 12–13 for more activities on this text.

Have a go!

Read the biography on the opposite page and answer these questions.

1 How many sisters does Lauren Child have?

....

2 What jobs did her parents do?

....

3 Did she have any training in art? If so, what was it?

....

....

4 What job did Lauren do before she began writing and illustrating?

....

5 How does she get her ideas for what her characters say?

....

6 Which two language features help us to know that this is a biography?

....

....

7 What would change if this were an autobiography?

....

....

Reading and writing challenge

1 Read some other types of biographical text, for example in a fan magazine, a sports or theatre programme, on the internet or in the obituary column in a newspaper. Note the similar features.

2 Write a short biographical piece about someone you know well. It might be a person or even a pet! But remember – try to get your facts right and don't write anything unkind or inappropriate.

Persuasion

Key facts

Persuasive text uses a number of techniques to influence the reader.

It might include arguments for or against something, with reasons, examples and extra information. It may appeal directly to the reader, using powerful, positive language. **Alliteration** or humour might help to draw the reader in, or a picture might tug at the heartstrings. Some writers use a catchy slogan or even poetry.

Model text

Are you bored with the same old places?
Tired of the same old faces?

Do you long for an adventure that's
OUT OF THIS WORLD?

Then this is YOUR lucky day!

YOU have been chosen out of thousands of young hopefuls to receive this offer of a lifetime.

For the greatly reduced price of only 1000 Dittos, you can book your place with

VANTAGE VACATIONS

Venturing aboard the Venus Voyager

Shooting past the stars

Perusing the planets

Your friends will never have seen holiday photos like these!

Places are limited so
DON'T DELAY – APPLY TODAY

Have a go!

Read the persuasive text on the opposite page and answer these questions.

1 How does the author make the reader feel they are special?

....

....

2 Why does the author choose to use the phrase 'OUT OF THIS WORLD'?

....

....

3 List two other features of persuasive text the author uses in this example?
Make sure you include quotations from the text.

a ....

....

b ....

....

4 Do you think this is a powerful piece of persuasive text? Explain your answer.

....

....

....

Reading and writing challenge

1 Find other examples of persuasion in everyday life, such as
television adverts, posters, leaflets. Decide which work and
which do not. Think of reasons for this. Does the style, content
or language depend on the audience?

2 Think of a place you have visited, or maybe somewhere you
would like to visit one day, and write a persuasive advert or
invitation, based on the example opposite, to encourage
other people to visit.

Make sure you include as many of the persuasive features as
possible to create a really effective text.

Discussion

Key facts

In a **discussion text**, the writer presents arguments and information from various **viewpoints**. Sometimes the writer simply puts forward the **facts**; at other times, the writer's viewpoint is clear and the text ends with some advice or a suggestion.

In a discussion text, the points are clearly grouped and **phrases** such as *on the other hand*, *however* and *in contrast to this* are used to introduce the differing points of view.

Model text   To see or not to see? That is the question!

Recently, I was asked, 'Which do you prefer – reading the book or watching the movie?' I had to think about that one.

I've always loved a good read. I was brought up surrounded by books and I remember times when I couldn't wait for it to be bedtime, not because I wanted to sleep, far from it, but because Enid Blyton, my favourite author at the time, had left the brothers and sisters Philip, Jack, Dinah, Lucy-Ann (and Kiki the parrot) in a cliffhanger of a situation on the Island of Adventure! For many years I have enjoyed that escape into a world of a book that has allowed me to build up a thousand pictures in my head.

On the other hand, I also love films. I love going to the cinema, or settling down on the sofa to watch a great story unfold. It's what rainy afternoons are made for! Once again, I am drawn into a magical world of make-believe. It's wonderful to see the locations; the scenery; the amazing actors making every scene come to life. I have watched movies that I didn't want to finish and others that have compelled me to watch them again and again.

However, the problem arises for me when a good book is turned into a film.

I have found that reading the book first can ruin the movie, and seeing the movie first leaves nothing for the imagination to do when reading the book. I have lost count of the number of times I have been disappointed when the pictures in my head didn't match up with the pictures on the screen. How can some directors get it so wrong? Don't they see the same things as me when they read the book? The answer to this is probably 'no'. That's the power of the imagination. The greatest issue for me is when they change the storyline. How dare they? The excuse – 'for cinematic purposes' – is really no excuse at all! A good story should stay a good story as far as I'm concerned.

So, reflecting on past experiences, if I had to make a decision between books and films, the answer must be that, while movies have given me great pleasure over the years, I still think you cannot beat the magical escape into a well-written book.

Have a go!

Read the magazine article on the opposite page and answer these questions.

1 What is the issue being discussed?

....

2 What reason does the writer give for looking forward to bedtime?

....

3 What does the writer say that reading a book allows her to do?

....

4 Which phrase lets the reader know that we are moving onto a different subject?

....

5 Why is the writer 'disappointed' when seeing the film *after* reading the book?

....

6 What do you think the phrase 'for cinematic purposes' means?

....

7 What is your opinion on this topic and why?

....

....

8 In your own words, what is the purpose of a discussion text?

....

....

Reading and writing challenge

1 Find other discussion texts and make a note of the language features the writers use. Build up a bank of useful words and phrases.

2 Write a short discussion text about two things you know something about.

> For example:
> Which is better: playing football or tennis? sun or moon?
> silver or gold? brothers or sisters?

Instructions

Key facts

Instructions tell the reader how to do something. The **imperative** form of the verb is always used, for instance *Sit* down, *Stand* up. Sometimes we call these 'bossy words'.

The layout of **instruction text** is very important. It should be clear and easy to follow. Each instruction should start on a new line and may also be introduced by a bullet point, number or **sequential language** such as *first*, *next*, *finally*, and so on.

Usually the steps are written in order and lead to a conclusion, but sometimes, like the ones below, they can be carried out in any order.

Model text — Explore nature with a ... magnifying glass

Follow these simple rules for using a magnifying glass or hand lens and you will see much more.

🔍 If you want to go on a bug hunt, get down on your hands and knees first. You won't be able to get a good look at a minibeast through your magnifying glass if you haven't spotted it first.

🔍 Move slowly and keep your shadow off your minibeast. Insect eyes can detect movement and your minibeast may hide if it sees you coming.

🔍 Whenever possible, steady the glass with both hands – you will see much clearer that way.

🔍 If you want to see under something but can't look directly, slip a small mirror under it and then use a magnifying glass on the reflection.

🔍 If you pick up a creature to have a closer look, try to put it back exactly where you found it. If you find a minibeast under a log, put it back under the same log – the next log might look the same to you and me but to an insect, it will be as different as someone else's bedroom.

🔍 Protect your lens from scratches – blow any sand or dust off before cleaning it gently with a soft cloth. Magnifying lenses aren't usually as tough as spectacles or binocular lenses.

🔍 Never leave your magnifying glass out in the sunshine. The heat from the sunlight shining through it could start a fire.

Have a go!

Read the instructions on the opposite page and answer these questions.

1 These instructions are:

rules ☐   directions ☐   a recipe ☐

2 What symbol is used instead of bullet points?

....

3 Where should you start reading, and how do you know this?

....

4 List the imperative verbs the writer uses in the first three rules.

....

5 Often it is vital that instructions are carried out in chronological order.
This is not the case here but, if it were, how would you make sure the
reader followed the sequence?

....

Reading and writing challenge 📄

1 Look for examples of instructions in everyday life. Sometimes they may
be very simple, consisting of one or two words, for example: STOP!
Sometimes they may involve detailed information, such as instructions
for how to set up your computer. Make a note of the different language
features used.

2 Write a list of instructions that you could
give to someone who is moving to a new
school. Your instructions will help them to
settle in and make new friends. Try not to
use the same imperative more than once.
You can use numbers, bullet points or
sequential language.

> For example: **1** Smile at people and
> show them that you are friendly.

Explanations

Key facts

An **explanation text**:

- explains a process

- tells the reader how or why something happens

- is always written in the present **tense**

- uses both time **connectives**, such as *first* and *next*, and causal connectives, such as *because* and *so*

- may include other features such as subheadings, diagrams, questions and tables to make the meaning clearer.

Model text — Why do I have to go to bed? I'm not tired!

The average person sleeps for around eight hours a day. That's one third of your life. In other words, you sleep for about 122 days a year and a 75-year-old person will have slept for about 25 years!

So, why do we sleep? It seems like a big waste of time!

Sleep is important for two main reasons:

1 It provides vital rest-time that helps the body to recover from everything that has happened to it during the day. While the muscles are inactive, the body can repair, fight disease, grow and restore.

  If a person does not get enough sleep, they are often tired, grumpy and lacking in energy.

2 Sleeping allows us to dream, which is important for learning and memory. Dreams help us to make sense of the world.

Did you know that sleep has stages?

Sleep follows a regular cycle each night. There are two basic forms of sleep:

- rapid eye movement (REM) sleep

- non-rapid eye movement (NREM) sleep. This has four different levels.

Infants spend about 50% of their sleep time in REM and 50% in NREM, whereas adults spend 20% in REM and 80% in NREM.

Most dreaming happens during REM sleep and we enter REM about five times in every eight-hour period of sleep. Of course we don't remember most of these dreams.

Have a go!

Read the explanation on the opposite page and answer these questions.

1 How long has the average 75-year-old person spent asleep?

....

2 Explain the two main reasons why sleeping is good for us.

a ....

b ....

3 What does REM stand for?

....

4 On average, when and how often in the sleep pattern do dreams occur?

....

....

5 What tense is this explanation text in and why?

....

....

Reading and writing challenge 📰

1 Rainbows are amazing! When there is a really bright one in the sky, it is possible to see all seven colours. Sometimes you can even see a double rainbow.

Find two or three different explanations of how rainbows are formed.

Take note of the tense and the language features the writer uses.

2 Write a short explanation *for a younger child* on how rainbows are formed. Take your audience into account.

Recounts

Key facts

Newspaper articles are often **recounts** or a retelling of events. Other examples of recounts might include diary entries, local newsletters and blogs.

Recounts:

- use time **connectives**, such as *first, then, sometime later*
- are written in the past **tense**
- are written in **chronological** order.

Model text   PYTHON ESCAPES!

Fear and panic swept the town of Marwick as a mountain python escaped from its cage.

The zookeepers first noticed it was missing at dawn, when they went round with morning feeds. They raised the alarm and local police were given instructions on how to corner the snake if anyone reported a sighting.

Early in the day, the local school reported a possible sighting, but the zoo were not sure if they believed the stripy creature spotted in the playground really was the python.

Residents in nearby homes then thought they'd seen something slithery but, again, it disappeared before the police could follow it.

In the end, the zoo found the python in the farm area, where it had eaten all the rabbits and mice. So maybe it had never got out into the town at all.

Have a go!
Read the newspaper article above and answer these questions.

1 What had escaped from its cage?

....

2 What instructions were given to the police?

....

3 How do you think the schoolchildren felt when they thought they saw the stripy creature and why?

....

....

4 The author uses the term 'slithery' to describe the snake. Think of three other words to describe the python.

....

5 What tense is this article written in and why?

....

....

6 Write down three connecting words or phrases that show the passage of time in this recount.

....

Reading and writing challenge

1 Read some newspaper articles that give recounts of events that have happened recently. Make a note of the language features used.

2 Write a short, simple recount of something that has happened in your life during the last week.

> For example, if you went swimming at the weekend:
> *On Saturday morning, a ten-year-old boy from Sometown went swimming at the local pool …*

Remember to use the past tense and include connectives – words and phrases – to show the passage of time.

Journalists often exaggerate the details to make a more exciting newspaper article. Rewrite your recount, using exaggeration to make it more exciting for your readers.

> For example:
> *In the early hours of Saturday morning, a ten-year-old boy from Sometown made the terrifying journey to his local swimming pool in order to brave the icy waters. He was alone!*

Reports

Key facts

A **report** is a **non-fiction** text that provides information. Reports:

- are usually arranged in sections and / or **paragraphs**
- often have subheadings to make it easier to find the information
- include sections that can be read in any order
- are written in the past **tense**.

Model text Athletics: Track events

Track events take place on a running track. Athletics tracks are oval, with a field in the centre. Most tracks are 400 m long. The track itself is divided up into lanes, which are marked with lines so the athlete knows which lane is theirs. The surface of the track can be grass, rubberised material or a special kind of tar.

Sprints

Races over short distances (100 m, 200 m and 400 m) are called sprints. Each sprinter starts in a separate lane and they have to stay in their own lane for the whole race. Most professional athletes start the race with their feet in blocks and their hands on the track. When the starting gun is fired, they push out of the blocks and run as fast as they can to the finish line. Usain Bolt of Jamaica runs the 100 m and 200 m sprint.

Relay races

A relay team consists of four runners who run as a team. They take turns to run a certain distance, one runner passing the baton to his or her team mate and that person runs the next part of the race. Relay races are often the highlight of an athletics meeting. At the 2011 IAAF World Athletics Championships, the team of Nesta Carter, Michael Frater, Yohan Blake and Usain Bolt set a world record for the 4 × 100 m relay.

Middle- to long-distance races

Runners can also compete in 800 m, 1500 m and 3000 m races. There is also a 5000 m and 10 000 m event on the track. These races are slower than the sprint, but the athletes need to be fit to keep up their pace for the whole race.

The longest race is the marathon. A standard marathon is 42 km long and it is usually run on roads away from the stadium.

Have a go!

Read the information on the opposite page and answer these questions.

1 Which three aspects of running are covered in this text and why is it easy to find the answer?

   a ....

   b ....

   c ....

   ....

2 What shape is an athletics track?..

3 How far will you run if you run once around the track? ....

4 What is a sprinter?

   ....

5 Which country won the 4 × 100 m relay at the 2011 IAAF World Athletics Championships?

   ....

6 Which running event is not on the track? Explain why not.

   ....

   ....

Reading and writing challenge 📑

1 Become an expert! Find out about a sport, event or hobby that you are interested in and keep a research notebook. Include what you already know but also gather new information from the internet, books or TV programmes. It is also useful to talk to experts and make notes on what they tell you. Gather photographs and pictures as well.

2 Write a fact sheet about your sport, event or hobby, which could be shared with others. Remember to write in sections or paragraphs and include subheadings and illustrations.

Key facts

A book review:

- summarises the content of the book
- puts forward the point of view of the reviewer
- may or may not recommend the book to the reader.

The blurb on the back of the book:

- briefly outlines the content
- tries to persuade the reader to buy / read the book.

THE GREAT KAPOK TREE

A TALE OF THE AMAZON RAIN FOREST

by Lynne Cherry

> **Model text** | A review: *The Great Kapok Tree*
>
>
>
> Lynne Cherry is an exceptional writer and artist. She personally visited the Amazon rainforest to make sketches and get inspiration for the marvellous picture story. The book stresses the importance of saving the rainforests without sounding dull, or lecturing to us.
>
> The story is a simple one. A man who is sent to cut down a massive kapok tree gets tired and takes a nap. As he sleeps, snakes, butterflies, a jaguar and a sloth that all live in the forest surround him. They take turns to whisper in his ear and tell him about the horrible consequences of living in a world without forests. Finally an Indian child joins them and also whispers in the man's ear. When the man wakes up, he sees all the creatures around him and he has to make a decision about what to do. He decides to put down his axe and walk away.
>
> Enjoyed by millions of children worldwide and translated into several languages, this book is a well-written and beautifully illustrated gem that will add to any reader's collection.

> **Model text** | The blurb
>
> In the Amazon rainforest, a man is chopping down a great kapok tree. Exhausted from his labours, he puts down his axe and rests.
>
> As he sleeps, the animals who live in the tree plead with him not to destroy their world.

Read the texts above and answer these questions.

1 Who wrote the book?

    .... [1]

2 Who illustrated the book?

    .... [1]

3 How did the author get inspiration for this book?

    .... [1]

4   Read the texts on page 37 again. Write down two words or phrases from the review that show whether the reviewer liked the book or not.

(a) ....

....

(b) ....

....   [2]

5   Write down the phrase that shows us that the book is already popular.

....

....   [1]

6   What do you think the Indian child said to the man?

....

....   [1]

7   Why did the man 'put down his axe and walk away'?

....

....   [1]

8   The book has an important message. What is it?

....   [1]

9   What tense is the review written in?

....   [1]

10   Name two places where you might find a book review.

(a) ....

(b) ....   [2]

11   What is the purpose of a book review?

....

....   [1]

12 Where do you normally find the blurb of a book?

.... [1]

13 What is the purpose of the blurb?

....

.... [1]

14 Write down two main differences between the styles of the two texts.

(a) ....

....

....

(b) ....

....

.... [2]

15 Would you like to read this book? ....

Give three reasons for your answer.

(a) ....

....

....

(b) ....

....

....

(c) ....

....

.... [3]

Writing skills

Planning stories

Read the traditional story below. It is a simple tale and there are versions of this story all over the world, so you will probably have heard it before, although the names and the setting may be different.

The story follows the structure:

1 introduction   2 build-up   3 problem / action / issue

4 resolution   5 ending.

Once upon a time, there was a young girl called Cinderella who lived with her father, her stepmother and her two stepsisters. Her father was a weak man and could do nothing to stop the wicked stepmother and stepsisters mistreating poor Cinderella. She was forced to work day and night in the kitchen, cleaning and mending.

One day, an invitation arrived. The prince was holding a spectacular ball at the palace. Everyone in the household was invited, but, true to form, the wicked stepmother and her equally evil daughters would not allow poor Cinderella to attend. As she only had the rags she stood up in, she knew that there was no chance she could go to the ball.

On the night of the ball, a fairy godmother visited the house, waved her magic wand and gave Cinderella a wonderful dress, sparkling jewels, a pair of crystal shoes and a fine carriage and horses. She sent her off to the ball with strict instructions to be back by midnight. At the palace, the prince and Cinderella danced all night until the clock struck twelve and Cinderella fled from the ball, leaving a single crystal slipper behind.

For many weeks, the prince scoured the country in search of the beautiful girl, promising to marry the one whose dainty foot could fit into the crystal slipper. The stepsisters tried in vain to squeeze their feet into the shoe and were horrified when the prince asked to meet *all* the females in the house.

Cinderella was called from the kitchen and when she tried on the slipper, it fitted perfectly. The prince asked her to be his bride and, of course, she said yes. So, they lived happily ever after, much to the annoyance of the two wicked stepsisters, who were forced to clean and mend from morning until night.

Have a go! 📖

It is easy to box up a known story to give you a model for a new story.

Here is a boxed-up version of the story on the opposite page.

Original	Pattern	My new story
Cinderella – lives with father, stepmother and stepsisters. Badly treated. Forced to work day and night.	**Introduction** Main Character (MC) is introduced. Setting and background	
Invitation to ball arrives. Sisters will not let Cinderella go.	**Build-up** Something exciting is about to happen but MC is not allowed to be part of it.	
On night of the ball, fairy godmother transforms Cinderella and sends her to the ball. But – Cinderella has to leave and her slipper is left behind.	**Problem / action / issue** Just as the exciting thing is about to happen, something happens to enable MC to be part of it. But – there is a problem.	
Prince searches for Cinderella, promising to marry the person whom the slipper fits. Asks to see Cinderella.	**Resolution** There is a plan to give MC a reward.	
Slipper fits and the prince asks Cinderella to marry him. They marry and live happily ever after.	**Ending** MC gets reward and lives happily ever after.	

Using the pattern, plan a new story, deciding on:

- your main character – it could be a totally different type of character
- the setting – it could be modern day, set in school, at a club, and so on

- the background
- any other characters

- the main event
- the problem

- how the problem is solved
- the ending.

Keep your notes brief and to the point. Key words are all you need.

Openings and endings

There are many good ways to start and end a story. Here are some possible openers and endings, which you could use with your own stories. These examples are for the traditional story 'Goldilocks and the Three Bears'.

Story openers

- Once upon a time – but personalise it: *Once upon a mischievous time …*

- Question: *Who could possibly live in this house?*

- Start in the middle of the action and flash back: *Goldilocks began to drift into a warm and comfortable sleep. It had all begun when she had discovered this cute little cottage in the heart of the forest.*

- Start at the end and flash back: *As Goldilocks managed to get her breath back, she began to tell her mother all about her narrow escape.*

- Description: *The sun peered through the leaves, casting delicate shadows on the cosy cottage that nestled in the heart of the forest.*

- Action: *Goldilocks pushed the door open cautiously.*

- **Dialogue:** *'Ouchhhhh! This porridge is much too hot to eat,' squealed Baby Bear.*

- Sound effect: *Creee-eeeaak! The door of the cottage swung slowly open.*

Story endings

- The end – or is it?: *Daddy Bear stared thoughtfully at the trail of tiny footprints Goldilocks had left behind her.*

- Traditional – with a twist: *They all lived hungrily ever after.*

- Moral ending: *Goldilocks was so sorry that she went back the next day with a basket of delicious cakes for the Bear family.*

- Lesson: *Never leave your porridge unattended!*

- It had all been a dream – or had it?: *She woke up. What was that on her arm … porridge!*

- Cliffhanger: *She heard footsteps behind her …*

- A joke or a pun: *She couldn't BEAR to stay a minute longer!*

- The title: *So, that is how Goldilocks met the Three Bears!*

- Question: *Would she ever find that little cottage again? Did she want to?*

- Summary of feelings: *Goldilocks felt relieved as she ran into the safe arms of her mother.*

- Full circle: *As she ran through the woods, she spied another little cottage with the door ajar …*

- A twist in the tale: *Goldilocks screamed! The bears turned and ran for their lives.*

- Unfinished: *… but that's another story!*

Can you think of any more?

Have a go!

1 Look back at your own story plan on page 41. It begins with the main character introduced in the setting.

Try two different ways of opening your story, using the suggestions on the opposite page. Continue on a separate sheet of paper if you need to.

a ....

....

b ....

....

2 The story on page 41 ends with the main character getting her reward and living happily ever after. Write two different endings for that story, using the suggestions on the opposite page and above. Continue on a separate sheet of paper if you need to.

a ....

....

b ....

....

Reading challenge

Look for exciting openings and endings in books and films and make a note of them in an author's notebook. You never know when they might come in useful.

Settings and characters

> ### Key facts
>
> The **setting** is the time and place in which the story takes place.
>
> The **characters** are the people (or animals, monsters, robots, and so on) who appear in the story.
>
> By choosing interesting settings and exciting characters, it is possible to create a great story.
>
> But you have to describe these to your reader. You have to paint the scenes with your words and make your characters come to life, not just with descriptions, but with what they say and how they move and react to people and situations.

Have a go!

1 Read this description.

> ### Model text
>
> Deep in a dark black space. Dank and dark, bleak and black. Is there any light at all? Yes, there's a piercing white light ahead: could it be the mouth of a cave, or the light at the end of the tunnel? It's a tiny relief compared with this overwhelming blackness, this damp chilling darkness, enveloping everything. What are the sounds? A drip of moisture from the roof, falling into a puddle in the rough ground underfoot. But otherwise there is just silence, leaving nothing to hear, as well as nothing to see. Where on earth am I?

a Highlight or underline all the adjectives in the description above.

Notice how the author uses:

- **alliteration** – deep, dark, dank
- contrasts – light and dark
- a cliffhanger at the end
- questions to draw the reader in
- sounds

b Picture an interesting setting in your mind. It is good to use somewhere you have been or seen in a film or a book or in photographs. Write a short description of the setting, making it real for the readers.

c Now try a contrasting one. If your first setting was dark and mysterious and a little bit scary, make the second one lively, vibrant, colourful and exciting, or the other way round. Again, relate it to somewhere you are familiar with.

2 Read this passage.

> ### Model text
>
> 'What are you two doing here?' snapped Miss Squeers. 'How dare you enter my room uninvited? If I had wanted to see your miserable little faces I would have sent for you. Get out now!'
>
>
>
> Miss Squeers raised her bony finger sharply and pointed at the open door. She glared over the top of her metal-rimmed glasses, her piercing grey eyes like lasers boring into Mia and Zina.
>
> 'B-b-but we just wanted to …' stammered Mia, her whole body shaking with fear as she clung on tightly to her best friend's hand. She was already small for her ten years but suddenly she felt the size of an ant. An ant that was about to be trodden on.
>
> 'I don't care what you wanted. GET OUT!' bellowed Miss Squeers, her wispy grey hair shaking with rage.

a What have we learnt about Miss Squeers from this passage – her appearance and her character? Notice how some of the information is given directly while some can be inferred from what she says, how she says it and how she acts towards other characters.

b The characters are contrasting, which is a technique that is often used. Think of two contrasting characters and jot down a few things about them. Think of good words to describe how they speak or move.

c Write a short passage, like the one above, that helps the reader know what your characters are like. Notice that the passage does *not* include a long list of descriptions like this: *Miss Squeers was a very strict lady. She was 62 years old. She had grey hair and wore metal-rimmed glasses. She …*

Reading challenge

Make a note of any good characters you come across in books, films or in real life and jot them down in your author's notebook. Keep a list of great words to use instead of *said* or *walked*.

Adding detail

Key facts

It is important to include detail in your writing, but it is also important to use the right amount of detail.

Too much 'flowery' description in a **recount**, such as a newspaper report, can get in the way of the facts.

> For example:
> The tall, burly policeman stood in his smart, crisp uniform, surveying the scene of the tragically uprooted old tree that had been viciously torn out of the earthy ground by the terrifying, torturous tornado.

Whereas, a lack of detail in a story can make it bland, boring and hard to visualise.

> For example:
> Jack was quite young. He walked down the road. When he got to the shop it was very busy so he started to walk home. He saw a group of older children. They spoke to him. They took his money.

It is also important to remember the **audience** for the piece of writing.

Sometimes it would be confusing for a younger child to have too much detail, but annoying for an adult to have not enough detail!

Here are four points to keep in mind:

Whether you are writing **fiction** or **non-fiction**, it is important to add detail when it:

- improves the writing

- helps to make the meaning clearer

- allows the text to achieve its purpose

- is appropriate for the audience.

Have a go! 📃

1 This piece has too much detail. Highlight the bits that are needed then rewrite the piece, making it more appropriate.

Sita Achari, who was eleven, walked through the familiar, green, leafy, tree-filled forest towards the old, dilapidated, empty cottage where she had arranged to meet her two wonderful, lovely best friends, Annie Mountford and Lou Yapp, who were both eleven years of age. The green leaves were swaying and waving in the gentle breeze and the spongy, mossy ground was soft, springy and lovely under her feet. After she had been walking for 27 minutes, in the distance, set among the trees, in a small clearing where there weren't any trees and sun was able to shimmer and shine down from the sky, she saw the old, dilapidated, empty cottage and her two wonderful, lovely best friends standing in the sunlight.

2 This information text hasn't got enough detail to be useful. Rewrite the piece, adding the appropriate amount of detail. You could research some information and use some specific language or give examples where necessary.

There are lots of fish in the world. There are big ones and small ones, dull ones and brightly coloured ones. You can find them in all types of places that have got water. Some people like to catch fish for different reasons. Some people keep some types of fish at their houses. Fish are different from other creatures.

Reading challenge

1 Read the passages above and your rewritten versions to someone else. Ask them which they prefer and why.

2 Look for examples of writing that include just the right amount of detail – they may be a newspaper report, a set of instructions or a story. Notice how important it is to get the amount of detail right.

Organisation and paragraphing

Key facts

Whether you are writing **fiction** or **non-fiction**, it is important to organise your work so that it makes sense to the reader.

Some writing needs to be in **chronological** order – starting at the beginning, moving through a logical sequence until it gets to the end.

Some texts are **non-chronological** – it doesn't matter what order you read them in.

Here's a brief guide to help you with organisation and planning:

Fiction

- Stories: Usually chronological; split into **paragraphs**; paragraphs are often linked with adverbial **phrases**, such as *The next day ...*, or **connectives**, such as *however*
- Stories often have: introduction; build-up; action / problem; resolution; ending
- Some stories use a flashback technique – they start at the end or the middle and then move back to what led up to this point
- Some stories are written in strands, for example following the same story from the points of view of different characters
- Stories can be written in many different styles or **genres**, such as historical
- Some stories are short and concise; longer ones are organised into chapters.

Non-fiction

- **Recount:** Tells the reader about events; usually chronological; answers the questions *who, when, where, what* and *why*; arranged in paragraphs using adverbial phrases or connectives to link them (see above)
- **Report:** Gives information that can be read in any order; non-chronological; arranged in sections, often with headings and subheadings
- **Instructions and procedures:** Tell the reader what to do; usually chronological; often arranged in sections with subheadings; may use numbering, bullet points or language such as *first, next*; may include diagrams or pictures
- **Explanation:** Describes how or why something happens; usually chronological although not always; often arranged in paragraphs, sections or bullet points with subheadings; often uses diagrams or pictures
- **Persuasion:** Sets out to influence or convince the reader; an opening statement followed by information in paragraphs or sections; includes details and extra information to make the reader think in the same way as the writer; often ends with a concluding paragraph or recommendation
- **Discussion:** Puts both sides of an argument; can be arranged in paragraphs as a 'for' point followed by the 'against' point, and so on, or all the 'for' points followed by all the 'against' points; usually ends with a summary or a recommendation.

Have a go!

Below are several pieces of text taken from an explanation, some instructions and a persuasive text. Draw lines, as in the example, to show which text each extract is from, then write the texts out in full, making sure the sentences are in the correct order and that they make sense. Add any other features you feel are appropriate, for example a subheading, numbering or bullet points.

One chamber is used to store the water.

I want to write to you about the polar bears you keep in your zoo.

They need to swim and catch fish from the sea.

Put the spaceship into gear.

Put on your super spacesuit.

The water is released from one chamber into the other by pressing a special valve at the top.

I think it is important for them to live in their own habitat for a number of reasons.

EXPLANATION

INSTRUCTIONS

PERSUASIVE TEXT

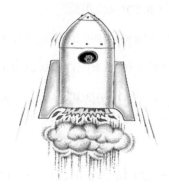

The special feature of this kettle is that it has two chambers.

They are suited to much colder climates.

Secondly, they need to be active.

Fasten your seat belt.

Count down and lift off!

The other chamber heats the water.

Climb into the pilot's seat.

Firstly, it has been so hot this summer, they must really be suffering.

A step-by-step guide

Reading challenge

Look at a selection of texts and spot all their different features.

Audience and purpose

Key facts

Whenever you are planning any piece of writing, start by asking yourself two questions:

1 What is the purpose of this type of writing?

> For example: is it to instruct, to entertain, to persuade, to give information?

2 Who is the **audience** for this type of writing?

Yes, your teacher might have asked you to do it, but who is this type of writing aimed at?

> For example, if it is a story, is it for a young child, someone your age, or an older reader?

If it is a set of **instructions**, is it for adults?

If it is a **recount**, is it for the school newsletter, for parents to read?

(See examples of different text types in the Reading genres chapter, pages 6–39.)

Once you have established these two important facts, it makes it much easier to get the style, features and organisation of the writing correct.

For example:

- The task: Write a letter to persuade the local government to provide more recycling facilities

- Audience: The local government

- Purpose: To persuade – to put across my point of view, strongly but politely

- Format: A letter

- Style: Formal – I want them to take notice of me

- Language: Persuasive – giving reasons and further details, appealing to emotions

- Organisation: Opening **paragraph**, to introduce my topic, so they know why I am writing; paragraphs on each point; concluding paragraph and recommendation.

Have a go!

Write a persuasive letter to the local government, including several reasons why they should provide recycling facilities, for example:

- it is better for the environment

- there would be less rubbish lying around

- everyone could get involved

- it will encourage people to think about the future.

Think about the structure and layout of your letter, paying particular attention to the opening and closing.

Remember to be strong, but formal and polite, backing up reasons with facts and information. Use persuasive language (see pages 24–25).

Writing challenge

A dragon has moved into the area! Choose one item from each box and write an appropriate piece. For example, you might want to write a letter to parents to inform them about the dragon, or a story to entertain a six-year-old about a dragon at school.

Audience	**Purpose**	**Format**
A six-year-old	To entertain	Story
The headteacher	To inform	Letter
Parents	To persuade	Poem
Local residents	To instruct	A newsletter article
A friend	To recount	A dragon fact sheet

How much can you remember? Test 2

1 Write down one key feature for each of these kinds of writing.

(a) Play-script .... [1]

(b) Direct speech .... [1]

(c) Reported speech .... [1]

(d) Story .... [1]

(e) Instructions .... [1]

(f) Advert .... [1]

(g) Autobiography .... [1]

(h) Biography .... [1]

(i) Explanation .... [1]

(j) Recount .... [1]

2 What is a setting?

....

....

....

....

.... [1]

3 What is a character?

....

....

....

.... [1]

4 Give one example of when you should NOT include too much descriptive
language.

....

.... [1]

5 What is a paragraph?

....

.... [1]

6 Why is it important to think about the audience when you are writing?

....

.... [1]

7 What is the difference between fiction and non-fiction?

(a) Fiction .... [1]

(b) Non-fiction .... [1]

8 Give two examples of an adverbial clause to finish this sentence:
I saw Joe …

(a) ....

(b) .... [2]

9 Which is your favourite type of text to write and why?

....

....

....

.... [1]

10 Write down three good words or phrases to describe each of the following.

    (a) an old tree .... [1]

    (b) a river .... [1]

    (c) the sky at night .... [1]

    (d) a mountain .... [1]

    (e) a tasty meal .... [1]

11 Write a descriptive sentence about each of the above nouns, using two or three of your words.

For example: The gnarled branches of the ancient tree snatched at the boy's clothing as he crept silently through the darkening forest.

    (a) ....

        .... [1]

    (b) ....

        .... [1]

    (c) ....

        .... [1]

    (d) ....

        .... [1]

    (e) ....

        .... [1]

12 Write three different opening paragraphs for an adventure story set on a mysterious island at night.

    (a) Begin with a setting description. [1]

    (b) Begin with some dialogue. [1]

    (c) Begin with action. [1]

13 Write three powerful phrases or slogans to persuade people to buy:

    (a) a new chocolate bar

    For example: The creamiest chocolate – a smile in every bite

    ....

    ....

    ....   [1]

    (b) a fast car

    ....

    ....

    ....   [1]

    (c) the latest item of sports equipment

    ....

    ....

    ....   [1]

14 Make a list of five words to use instead of 'said' if the speaker is:

    (a) grumpy ....   [1]

    (b) nervous ....   [1]

    (c) scary ....   [1]

15 Make a list of five words to use instead of 'went' if the person is:

    (a) grumpy ....   [1]

    (b) nervous ....   [1]

    (c) scary ....   [1]

Sentence structure and punctuation

Nouns

> ### Key facts
>
> A **noun** is the name of a person, place or thing.
>
> A noun phrase is a string of words that acts like a noun in a **sentence**.
>
> A **collective noun** is a group or collection of people, animals or things.
>
> A **pronoun** – for example *he*, *she*, *his*, *her* – replaces the noun.

Have a go!

1   Complete each phrase correctly using one of the collective nouns below.

flock	herd	pack	shoal	crew
school	collection	fleet	litter	swarm

a   a .... of cows

b   a .... of wasps

c   a .... of cards

d   a .... of stamps

e   a .... of birds

f   a .... of puppies

g   a .... of fish

h   a .... of ships

2   Circle the best word to complete each collective noun phrase.

a   a flock / string of beads

b   a band / gang of musicians

c   a set / bundle of sticks

d   a bunch / beach of bananas

e   a bouquet / smell of flowers

f   a herd / swarm of elephants

g   a crow / crowd of people

h   a bride / pride of lions

Writing challenge

Try inventing some collective nouns of your own. Choose words that describe the nouns well. For example: a float of crocodiles, an annoyance of mobile phones, a circle of mathematicians.

a   a .... of teachers

b   a .... of sunflowers

c   a .... of pop-stars

d   a .... of cars

Nouns may be divided according to their gender.

Nouns that refer to males are masculine nouns.

a boy

Nouns that refer to females are feminine nouns.

a girl

Nouns that refer to either a male or a female have a common gender and are called common nouns.

a teacher

This is a neuter noun. Neuter means without gender.

a book

Have a go!

1 Write the nouns in the correct place in the table.

niece	husband	fork	pupil	uncle	bull
guest	nun	bride	camera	traveller	hotel
doctor	friend	lioness	prince	car	patient

Masculine	Feminine	Common	Neuter

Reading challenge

Make a list of all the pronouns you can think of.

Read a passage from a favourite book. Look out for how the author uses pronouns in place of nouns, proper nouns (names of people or places, which are spelt with a capital letter) or noun phrases. What effect does this have?

Keep a tally chart and see which appears most often. Make a note of which ones are 'possessive' (show belonging), for example 'his', 'her'.

Verbs

Key facts

Verbs can be:

- action or 'doing' words, for example: *to run, bring, talk, learn*

- 'being' words, for example: *to be, exist*

- 'occurrence' words, for example: *to happen, become.*

They can be used in many different forms:

- **Imperative** verbs are used for giving orders or instructions.

- **Passive verbs** are used for formal language.

Examples:

<table>
<tr>
<td>

You use imperatives to give an order or instruction:

- Shut the door! Turn left! Put it outside!

You therefore find imperatives in any kind of **instruction text**, for example: recipes, rules for games, directions.

</td>
<td>

You use passive verbs to describe actions 'being done':

- Active – I kicked the ball into the goal.

- Passive – The ball was kicked into the goal.

You use the passive for **explanations**, some **recounts** or in **formal writing**.

</td>
</tr>
</table>

This will help you to spot the difference between instructions and explanations.

Have a go!

1 Circle the imperatives in this set of instructions.

a Draw some monkeys on cardboard.

b Give them curled tails to swing from.

c If you make a mistake, rub it out and try again.

d Colour the monkeys in bright colours.

e Cut them out.

f Go carefully round the corners.

g Join them together.

h Hang them on the end of your bed, or over a baby's cot.

3 Highlight the passive verbs in this explanation about bread making.

a The cereal is sown in the spring and harvested in the autumn.

b The seeds are then separated from the ears of corn.

c The seeds are ground to make flour.

d The flour is transported to the bakery.

e The flour is then used to bake bread.

f The bread is sold to us through bakeries and supermarkets.

4 Rewrite the explanation above using active verbs.

The first sentence has been rewritten for you.

a We sow the cereal in the spring and harvest it in the autumn.

b ....

c ....

d ....

e ....

f ....

Writing challenge
Try turning the statements in Question 3 into a set of instructions.

The first one has been done for you.

1 Sow the cereal in the spring and harvest it in the autumn.

2 ....

3 ....

4 ....

5 ....

6 ....

Adverbs and adjectives

An **adverb** usually tells us more about a **verb**. There are different types of adverb.

A girl was *quietly* reading her book.	A few minutes *later* she stopped.	She went *outside*.

An adverb of *manner* answers the question 'How?'	An adverb of *time* answers the question 'When?'	An adverb of *place* answers the question 'Where?'

Comparative and superlative adjectives

When we compare two **nouns** we use a comparative **adjective**.

When we compare more than two nouns we use a superlative adjective.

My face is *muddy*.	My face is *muddier*.	My face is the *muddiest*.
↑	↑	↑
This is the *root adjective*.	*Comparative adjectives* often end with *-er*.	*Superlative adjectives* often end with *-est*.

Have a go!

1 Circle the adverb in each sentence. Say if it is an adverb of *manner (m)*, *time (t)* or *place (p)*.

a Mrs Smith answered sharply. ☐   **b** Our visitors arrived yesterday. ☐

c Will you be there? ☐   **d** We seldom see each other. ☐

e I turned the box around. ☐   **f** I slept very badly. ☐

g Tomorrow I am going swimming. ☐   **h** We looked everywhere for the key. ☐

2 Match up each adverb with the verb it best describes and then write each pair in a sentence.

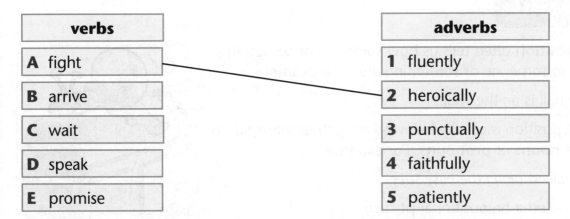

verbs
A fight
B arrive
C wait
D speak
E promise

adverbs
1 fluently
2 heroically
3 punctually
4 faithfully
5 patiently

3 Complete this table of adjectives. Take care with the spellings.

Root adjective	Comparative adjective	Superlative adjective
tall	taller	
wide		widest
dry		driest
	sharper	
		wettest
	happier	

Writing and reading challenge 📝

Not all adjectives perform in this way. Isn't that typical!

Sometimes the word changes completely. For example: good – better – best.

Or sometimes it is necessary to use a phrase, such as *more beautiful* or *most beautiful.*

1 Write the comparative and superlative forms of the following adjectives:

   a bad – .... – ....

   b private – .... – ....

   c far – .... – ....

   d many – .... – ....

2 There are some adjectives that don't need comparatives and superlatives because something either *is* or *is not*. For example: dead, unique, correct.

   Can you think of any others?

Prepositions

Key facts

A **preposition** often tells us how someone or something relates to someone or something else. For example:

- The snail is *on* the wall.

The preposition is usually followed by further information such as **nouns** or **pronouns**. For example:

- He walked *along the busy street*.

This is called a prepositional **phrase**.

Some prepositions can be added to a verb to change the meaning completely. For example: *to look* means 'to see / employ sight', but:

- to look *up* means 'to research in a book'   • to look *up to* means 'to admire someone'

- to look *down on* means 'to think you are better than someone else'

Have a go!

1 Circle the preposition in each sentence.

a The child stared curiously at the lady.

b There were four eggs in the nest.

c The man rowed the boat across the river.

d The garage is behind the house.

e The children strolled through the woods.

f The horse jumped over the fence.

g The beetle was under the rock.

h Lots of houses were destroyed during the hurricane.

2 Complete these sentences with an appropriate preposition.

You can only use each preposition once.

For example: The ant scurried quickly <u>along</u> the branch.

a The cake was shared .... the two children.

b The young boy crept .... his friend.

c The swimmer dived .... the pool.

d The tree stood .... the house.

3 Each of these verbs uses a preposition. Put each one into a sentence to show its new meaning when used with the preposition.

a give up ....

b look after ....

c stand out ....

d get up ....

e run out of ....

f look into ....

g give in ....

h run into ....

Writing challenge

This poor man seems to be having a very strange day! Read the following text.

It was a windy day and a branch of a tree fell <u>on</u> the man's head. He decided to move, so he walked quickly <u>into</u> the busy road and sat down <u>under</u> a park bench. Just at that moment a rabbit ran <u>over</u> him. He followed it <u>above</u> the trees but he soon got tired so he sat down and rested <u>in</u> the river. It was beginning to get dark and an owl screeched loudly <u>inside</u> his ear. He got up and headed <u>away from</u> his home. He came to a sign that said 'Dangerous Animals. No Entry!' He turned and there, standing <u>next to</u> him, was an enormous lion.

Rewrite the passage, changing the underlined prepositions, so that the day sounds a little more realistic and a little less dangerous! Don't use the same preposition more than once.

Compound sentences

Key facts

A **clause** consists of two parts:

- the subject (who or what the clause is about)
- the predicate (the rest of the clause, which must include a verb).

A simple **sentence** consists of just one clause.

The wind   blew strongly.
subject   *predicate (including the verb 'blew')*

A **compound sentence** is made up of two or more clauses of equal weight, joined by simple **connectives** – *and, or, but, so*. These are both known as **main clauses**.

The wind blew strongly   so   the boat moved quickly.

These particular connectives are sometimes referred to as *co-ordinating conjunctions*.

In a compound sentence the conjunction always comes between the two clauses that it is joining. It is the glue that holds them together.

Have a go!

1 Underline the subject and circle the verb in each one-clause sentence.

For example: <u>The monkey</u> (pulled) a funny face.

a The boy walked over the bridge.   **b** The children entered the museum.

c Toby scored the winning goal.   **d** Sharks swim in the sea.

2 Underline the verbs in these sentences and say if each sentence has one or two main clauses.

a The sun shone and the wind blew. ☐

b The fox hunted for food in the forest. ☐

c I ate the curry and rice hungrily. ☐

d The story started in an exciting manner. ☐

e The shop was open but it had sold out of milk. ☐

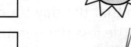

3 Join two simple sentences together, one from A and one from B, to make a compound sentence. Use an appropriate conjunction, remembering to make sure both clauses are of equal importance. You can join them in any combination you choose – there is no right or wrong way – but you can only use each clause once.

A	B
The sun was very hot.	The man stood still.
The boy ran across the road.	I felt sick.
The meal was disgusting.	There was a terrible noise.
The train was full.	Everyone complained.
The ball went through the window.	I went home.

a ....

b ....

c ....

d ....

e ....

Writing challenge 📄

When Stan writes in his diary, he often writes in simple sentences. Can you make this passage sound better by joining some of the sentences together to make compound sentences? You may wish to keep some sentences as simple sentences to add variety.

I wanted to go to the park. It was cold. I put on a coat. I asked my brother if he wanted to come. We went outside. We started to walk down the road. The pavement was icy. I nearly fell over. We arrived at the park. My brother ran on ahead. He ran towards the river. I shouted at him. He did not stop. He jumped. He landed on a thick layer of ice. He slipped. He fell over. It looked so funny. I told him off. It was a dangerous thing to do. He could have gone through the ice into the cold water.

Complex sentences

Key facts

A **clause** is a group of words containing a verb that may be used as a whole, simple **sentence**, or part of a sentence.

A **complex sentence** is made up of more than one clause.

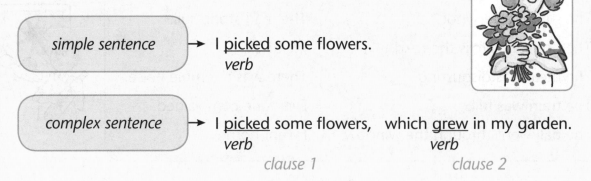

> *simple sentence* → I <u>picked</u> some flowers.
>   *verb*

> *complex sentence* → I <u>picked</u> some flowers,   which <u>grew</u> in my garden.
>   *verb*   *verb*
>   *clause 1*   *clause 2*

In complex sentences, there is a *main clause* and one or more *subordinate clauses*.

> After he had won the race, the boy fell off his bike.
>   *subordinate clause*   *main clause*

The **main clause** is complete on its own:

- The boy fell off his bike.

The subordinate clause contains the **connective** and does not make sense on its own:

- After he had won the race.

Sometimes a connective and subordinate clause can be dropped into the middle of the main clause:

> The older boys, <u>who were much more sensible,</u> prepared the barbecue.
>   *subordinate clause*

- 'The older boys prepared the barbecue' is the main clause and makes sense on its own.

- 'who were much more sensible' is the subordinate clause and does not make sense on its own.

Have a go!

Make complex sentences from the information you are given in three different ways, using three different connectives. The *m* shows which should be the main clause; the *s* shows which should be the subordinate clause.

For example:
The car drove along the road. *(m)* The car had a flat tyre. *(s)*

- The car drove along the road even though it had a flat tyre.

- Despite having a flat tyre, the car drove along the road.

- The car, although it had a flat tyre, drove along the road.

1   The fence stayed up in the high wind. *(m)* The fence was rickety and old. *(s)*

2   Suki and Suraj got full marks in the test. *(m)* Suki and Suraj had worked hard. *(s)*

3   The man packed up the stall. *(m)* The man had sold all his vegetables. *(s)*

Writing challenge

Complex sentences can also be created using a 'conditional clause'.

For example:
If I hurry, I will not miss the bus.
Unless you come closer, you will not be able to see.

'If I hurry' and 'Unless you come closer' are the conditionals, but they are still subordinate clauses because they contain verbs but don't make sense on their own.

Write five sentences that contain conditional clauses.

1   ....

   ....

2   ....

   ....

3   ....

   ....

4   ....

   ....

5   ....

   ....

Commas

Key facts

The **comma** might be small, but it is very important.

It allows time for a slight pause in our reading, and helps the passage to make more sense.

It can be used in a number of ways:

1 *After* the subordinate clause in a **complex sentence** (see page 66)

> For example: Although he was only ten, David looked like a teenager.

2 *Before and after* some extra information – the subordinate clause – is dropped into a complex sentence (see page 66); this is using the commas like brackets – or parentheses

> For example: David, who was only ten, looked like a teenager.

3 *After* a **connective** at the start of a sentence

> For example: However, Lisa had made up her mind that she would not go.

4 *After* an **adverb** at the start of a sentence

> For example: Cautiously, the explorer made his way into the cave.

5 *Between* the words in a list (but not before the *and*)

> For example: I went to the market where I bought an orange, a banana, a mango and a plum.

6 *Between* two or three adjectives in a sentence

> For example: The hungry bear roamed through the dark, menacing forest.

Have a go!

Write out these sentences, adding commas in the right places.

1 Mrs Grisly the scariest teacher in the school stormed into the classroom.

....

....

....

2 She was a mean-looking individual with a small beaky nose.

....

....

....

3 She wore a grey suit flat shoes thick stockings and a small pair of glasses on the end of her nose.

....

....

4 Menacingly she glared at the children in front of her.

....

....

5 Only the brave and that was not very many of them dared to meet her gaze.

....

....

6 However even the brave ones soon began to tremble and look away.

....

....

Writing challenge 📄

Write the next part of this story. Try to use each of the sentence structures above, making sure to put the commas in the correct places.

Apostrophes

> ### Key facts
>
> We sometimes use an **apostrophe** to show ownership – that means 'belongs to someone'.
>
> When there is only one owner, we write the 's after the **noun** that is the owner.
>
> - For example: the boy's coat = the coat that belongs to the boy.
>
> But when there is *more than one* owner so that the noun already ends in an *s*, we don't usually add another *s*, we just put the apostrophe at the end of the noun.
>
>
>
> - For example: the girls' bags = the bags belonging to the girls.
>
> However, if the *single* noun already ends in an *s*, follow the same rule as for plurals – don't add another *s*, just put the apostrophe on the end.
>
> - For example: Mr Jones' house, James' pen.

Have a go!

1 Complete the table below.

Longer form	Shorter form using an apostrophe
the cave belonging to the dragons	the dragons' cave
the saddles belonging to the horses	
the car belonging to the man	
the eggs belonging to the birds	
the computer belonging to the teacher	
	the doctors' surgery
	the shops' car park
	the zebra's mane
	the footballers' kitbags

2 Rewrite the passage below using the shortened form for the underlined words. Make sure you put the apostrophes in the correct place, and add *s* where necessary.

The mouse belonging to James was always escaping! He would jump over the fence into the garden belonging to Mr Jones, sneak past the kitchen window belonging to Old Sally and nip through the gate belonging to Mr Patel. He always forgot to shut it! As soon as he was free, the mouse would head for the school where James was. He would run through the car park belonging to the teachers, creep inside the front door belonging to the school and make straight for the classroom belonging to James. Luckily, the teacher belonging to James always laughed and said, 'Isn't it lovely to see someone so keen to come to school!'

....

....

....

....

....

....

....

Writing challenge

We also use apostrophes when we shorten words and miss out letters.

For example: didn't = did not

could've = could have

These are called *contractions* and we usually use them in informal writing or speech and dialogue. It is a very chatty style of writing.

> For example:
>
> 'He didn't know that he could've got there earlier,' said Jo.

List as many contractions as you can and write what they are short for. Can you find more than 20?

Direct and reported speech

Key facts

There are two ways of writing the words people say:

Direct speech – using speech marks

Reported speech – reporting the words afterwards

'When does the bus go?' she asked.

'At half past eight,' he answered.

'Oh dear,' she wailed, 'that means I've missed it then.'

He cheered her up by saying, 'But there'll be another one along soon.'

She asked him about the time of the bus and he told her that it went at half past eight. She was upset and said that she must have missed it, but he reassured her by telling her that there would be another one along soon.

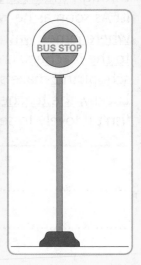

What are the differences between the two passages above?

Have a go!

Here is part of a play-script. Rewrite it first as direct speech, then as reported speech. Take care to use appropriate words instead of 'said'.

Model text

Jamelia: Hey! I want to show you something!

Amina: What is it?

Jamelia: I'm not telling you. It's a secret.

Amina: Where is it then?

Jamelia: Back home. Come round and I'll show you.

Writing challenge 📄

Read this passage from *Matilda* by Roald Dahl.

> **Model text**
>
> The Trunchbull's whole body and face seemed to swell up as though she was being inflated by a bicycle pump.
>
> 'I knew it!' she bellowed. 'I knew as soon as I saw you that you were nothing but a piece of filth! What is your father's job, a sewage-worker?'
>
> 'He's a doctor,' Nigel said, 'and a jolly good one. He says we're all so covered with bugs anyway that a bit of extra dirt never hurt anyone.'
>
> 'I'm glad he's not *my* doctor,' the Trunchbull said. 'And why, might I ask, is there a baked bean on the front of your shirt?'
>
> 'We had them for lunch, Miss Trunchbull.'
>
> 'And do you usually put your lunch on the front of your shirt, Nigel? Is that what this famous doctor father of yours has taught you to do?'
>
> 'Baked beans are hard to eat, Miss Trunchbull. They keep falling off my fork.'
>
> 'You are disgusting!' the Trunchbull bellowed. 'You are a walking germ-factory! I don't wish to see any more of you today! Go and stand in the corner on one leg with your face to the wall!'
>
> 'But Miss Trunchbull …'
>
> 'Don't argue with me, boy, or I'll make you stand on your head! Now do as you're told!'
>
> Nigel went.

Imagine you were in the class and witnessed this conversation. You are writing to a friend and telling them all about it. Rewrite the passage using reported speech. You could start with:

You'll never guess what happened today. Miss Trunchbull had a real go at this boy called Nigel. Her body and face seemed…

Using a range of punctuation

Key facts

Punctuation makes both **fiction** and **non-fiction** easier to read and understand.

Sometimes the information is clearer as a result of punctuation. For example:

The market cannot close because:

- local people rely on it for fresh food;
- farmers need somewhere to sell their goods;
- it is five miles to the nearest town.

Sometimes punctuation is the author's way of telling the reader how they want something to be read.

Silently, the boy crept into the cold, dark room. He froze. He looked around.

What was that lurking in the shadows?

No! It couldn't be! It was a…

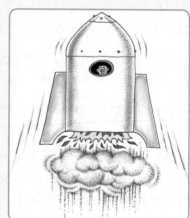

Below are some more examples of punctuation in sentences.

Read the amazing offer and circle the punctuation. Think about what the punctuation is doing and how it affects your reading and understanding.

Amazing offer!

Ever wanted to fly to the moon?

This is a chance for you – yes YOU! – to make your dream come true.

All you need to do is send your details, a photograph, a doctor's certificate and all your money to this address:

Big Con Promotions, 1a, Don't Do It Street, Toogoodtobetrue, UK.

'I had the time of my life!' (Mr Smith – a satisfied customer)
'It really was a dream come true!' (another satisfied customer)

Apply today and the dream is just beginning…

(If you don't hear back straight away, don't worry; we haven't forgotten you.)

Have a go!

Write a sentence for each of these examples of punctuation, making sure you use them appropriately.

1 ! (exclamation mark) ....

2 ? (question mark) ....

3 ... (dots) ....

4 , (comma) ....

5 ( ) (brackets) ....

6 – (dash) ....

7 ; (semi-colon) ....

8 : (colon) ....

Writing challenge 📄

Write a short advertisement (like the one opposite) for anything you choose, *appropriately* using as many different forms of punctuation as you can.

Award yourself marks for each example of punctuation you include:

capital letter = 1 mark   . = 1 mark

, = 1 mark   ? = 2 marks

! = 2 marks   : = 3 marks

; = 3 marks   ( ) = 4 marks

– = 4 marks   ... = 5 marks

But – be careful! The punctuation must be accurate and add to the meaning of the sentence.

1 Choose the best adjective to complete each simile.

quiet   slippery

(a) as .... as an eel

(b) as .... as a mouse   [2]

2 Rewrite these sentences, changing the verbs from passive to active.

(a) The tree was climbed by the girl.

....

....

....

(b) The apple was eaten by the boy.

....

....

....   [2]

3 Write whether each adverb is:

• an adverb of manner (m)

• an adverb of time (t)

• an adverb of place (p).

(a) soon   ☐

(b) everywhere   ☐   [2]

4 How many clauses are there in these sentences?

(a) The thunder roared and the rain fell.   ☐

(b) The old man sat down wearily.   ☐   [2]

5   Join these simple sentences to make a complex sentence, starting with the subordinate clause (s) and punctuating correctly.

(a) The boy was not tired. He had been up all night. (s)

    ....

    ....

    ....

(b) The sun was shining. The wind was cold. (s)

    ....

    ....

    ....   [2]

6   Rewrite this passage, punctuating it correctly.

There are ten items of punctuation missing.

> What have you got in your bag' asked Simeon
>
> Only a towel some swimming shorts and my money replied Matt.
>
> They walked around the corner and froze
>
> Unbelievably there in front of them stood a

....

....

....

....

....

....

....   [10]

Phonics and spelling

Vowel and consonant phonemes

> ### Key facts
>
> **Phonemes** are the smallest units of sound that you can hear in words. For example:
>
> c–a–t (3 phonemes)
>
> A phoneme can be made by one, two, three or four letters:
>
> m–o–p (3 phonemes)   sh–i–p (3 phonemes)
>
> h–<u>igh</u> (2 phonemes)   <u>eigh</u>–t (2 phonemes)
>
> ### Vowel phonemes
>
> The five **vowels** are *a, e, i, o* and *u*.
>
> They can be short vowels as in 'bag', 'beg', 'big', 'bog', 'bug', or long vowels. Some examples of long vowels are the sounds in 'rain', 'bean', 'die', 'coat' and 'moon'.
>
>
>
> A **grapheme** is the written form of the phoneme.
>
> Long vowel phonemes can be written in a number of ways and we have to choose the right grapheme to match the sound.
>
> | Long 'a' | | Long 'e' | | Long 'i' | | Long 'o' | | Long 'u' | |
> |---|---|---|---|---|---|---|---|---|---|
> | ay | day | e | be | i | find | o | no | u | use |
> | a–e | game | ee | deep | i–e | hide | ow | crow | o | to |
> | ai | pain | ea | stream | igh | light | oe | toe | oo | food |
> | eigh | eight | y | funny | y | by | oa | road | ew | blew |
> | ea | great | i | piano | e–e | eye | o–e | note | ough | through |
> | ei | reindeer | ie | thief | | | | | | |
> | | | ei | ceiling | | | | | | |
>
> ### Consonant phonemes
>
> In the alphabet, all letters that are not vowels are **consonants**.
>
> In the same way as vowel phonemes, consonant phonemes can be written in more than one way. For example:
>
> - c / k / ck / qu / ch: cat, kit, clock, quiet, choir
> - ch / tch: chat, catch
> - j / dj / dge: jig, adjective, bridge
>
> The more often you read and write words, the more likely you are to make the right choice in spelling.

Have a go!

1 Circle the correct spelling of each long vowel grapheme.

a The rays / rais from the sun can be dangerous.

b I will get my lorry to toe / tow you down the road.

c I have planted a lovely beech / beach tree in the garden.

d I blue / blew the froth off the top of my coffee.

e I will trigh / try to get there on time.

2 Choose the correct consonant graphemes to complete these words.

a something that tells the time   clo...................

b something that swims in water   fi.....................

c something that runs along the side
of a country road   di....................

d something that crosses over a river   bri...................

e a group of people who all sing together   ....oir

Writing and reading challenge

Suzie is always getting her spelling wrong. Can you help her? Write the text below with the correct spelling.

The mewn was hy in the skigh. An owl huted earily someware in the distanse. Thair was a smell of smoak and a straynje cracling sownd. Sam wated at the ej of the parque. Shood he gow on or shood he turn bak?

....

....

....

....

....

....

Common letter strings

Key facts

We often put a 'string' of two, three or even four letters together in a word to make a particular **phoneme** (sound) or **syllable** (part of a word).

Some of these strings may be added to the beginning or end of a word (see pages 84–85 on prefixes and suffixes), for example *dis* and *tion*, but some make up the main body of the word, for example *ould* in 'could' and 'should'.

It is helpful to look for common letter patterns or 'strings' in groups of words.

This can help us to remember their spellings.

dolphin
'ph' is a letter string

Have a go!

1 Sort the words in the box into sets according to their common letter patterns. There will be three words in each set. One set has been done for you.

boredom	examination	choir	pause	education	learn
conversation	freedom	hedge	character	saucer	ledge
search	wedge	author	early	kingdom	chemist

'dom' words	'...................' words	'...................' words
boredom freedom kingdom		

'...................' words	'...................' words	'...................' words

Some common letter strings can sound the same, for example: *ant* and *ent*.

arrog<u>ant</u>   obedi<u>ent</u>

2 Choose the correct letter strings to complete these words.

For example: arrog<u>ant</u>, obedi<u>ent</u>

a abund...........................

b intellig...........................

c extravag...........................

d magnific...........................

e ignor...........................

f viol...........................

g fragr...........................

h evid...........................

3 Match the words you completed to their meanings. Use a dictionary if you need to.

a ....: easily seen

b ....: very grand

c ....: plentiful

d ....: clever

e ....: spending a lot of money

f ....: sweet-smelling

g ....: not knowing much

h ....: very strong and rough

Reading challenge

Look out for common letter strings in your reading and start your own collection of 'word families' that go together.

Once you have a collection, invent some word games to play with friends, for example: word family bingo, word family snap, happy word families, word family dominoes, word family pairs.

Find the instructions for the original games and think how you could adapt them to use with groups of words. It's a fun way to learn spellings.

Spelling rules

> ### Key facts
>
> Spelling the English language can be very hard. There are so many things to remember. Sometimes it helps to learn some rules or, even better, make up some of your own!
>
> We do this by investigating what happens when we put certain letters together in words.
>
> For example: Why are there so many ways of spelling with *c* and *k*?
>
> > The king had been coaxing the cackling crowd into circles for what seemed like centuries.
>
> Sometimes the sound is *hard* as in 'cat' or *soft* as in 'century'. This can depend on where in the word the letters appear.
>
> ### Rules:
>
> 1 If you have a hard *c* sound at the *beginning* of the word:
>
> - before vowels *a*, *o* and *u* – use *c*: cat, cot, cut
> - before vowels *e* and *i* – use *k*: keg, keep, kit, kite.
>
> 2 If you have a hard *c* sound in the *middle* or *at the end* of the word or syllable:
>
> - usually use *ck*: rock, back, tickle, cackle
> - but sometimes use *ic*: music, picnic.
>
> 3 When do you use a soft *c* (*s* sound)?
>
> - before the vowels *e* and *i* at the beginning of words: certain
> - before the vowels *e* and *i* in the middle of words: musician.
>
> Another common spelling rule is:
>
> - *i* before *e* (when it makes the *ee* sound) except after *c*.
>
>
>
> shield
>
>
>
> ceiling

Have a go!

1 Write three words in each column.

hard c	soft c	ck	k
....	....	....	....
....	....	....	....
....	....	....	....

2 Fill in these *-ic* words.

For example: very sad: <u>tragic</u>.

a stretchy: e.....................

b very busy: h.....................

c like an idiot: i.....................

d common material: pl.....................

3 The ending *-ician* is often used for people's jobs. Write the names for these people.

a gives beauty treatments: b.....................

b works in politics: p.....................

c does magic tricks: m.....................

d tests your eyesight: op.....................

4 Follow the '*i* before *e* rule' and complete these words with *ie* or *ei*.

a shr.................k

b rec.................ve

c pr.................st

d f.................ld

e misch.................f

f p.................ce

g dec.................ve

h sh.................ld

i rel.................f

j conc.................t

k y.................ld

l bel.................ve

m rec.................pt

n gr.................f

o perc.................ve

Writing challenge 📑

Here's another spelling rule:

• When *-ar* follows *w* it sounds like *-or*.

• When *-or* follows *w* it sounds like *-er*.

Make a list of any words (ooh – there's one!) that follow the 'warm worm' rule.

Use a dictionary to help if you get stuck.

a warm worm

Prefixes and suffixes

Key facts

A **prefix** is a group of letters that goes in front of a **root word**. Prefixes change the meanings of words.

A **suffix** is a group of letters than can be added to the end of a root word to change its meaning or the way it is used.

For example:

- from *port*, meaning 'to carry' – you can build *transport, portable, transportable*

- from *sign*, meaning 'a mark' – you can build *resign, signing, resigning*.

These suffixes help turn words into different classes:

- Noun suffixes turn root words into nouns.
  For example: *-er, -ist, -ness, -ment*.

  drum – drummer
  cycle – cyclist
  happy – happiness
  argue – argument

- Adjective suffixes turn root words into adjectives.
  For example: *-ful, -less, -er, -est*.

  help – helpful   help – helpless
  big – bigger   big – biggest

- Verb suffixes turn root words into verbs.
  For example: *-en, -ing, -ed*.
  (These are sometimes known as **inflections**.)

  flat – flatten, flattening, flattened

- Adverb suffixes turn root words into adverbs.
  For example: *-ly*.

  truly   madly   deeply

Have a go!

1 These prefixes all help you build new words with new meanings:

    a *pre* means 'before' – so *preview* means ....

    b *re* means 'again' – so *replay* means ....

    c *im* means 'not' – so *impossible* means ....

2 Write a sentence using each of these words and explain what the prefix means:

   a night ....

      midnight ....

      mid means ....

   b clockwise ....

      anti-clockwise ....

      anti means ....

   c zero ....

      subzero ....

      sub means ....

3 Write down some other examples of words using the suffixes *-ness*, *-er*, *-ist* and *-ment*. Take care with spelling!

root word	-ness
dark	darkness

root word	-er
play	player

root word	-ist
art	artist

root word	-ment
astonish	astonishment

Writing challenge 📋

Sometimes, when a word is modified, it is necessary to double the consonant.

For example: hop – hopping; run – running; hid – hidden; sag – saggy.

Find some examples of these and work out a rule that explains when it is necessary to double the consonant.

Synonyms and antonyms

> ### Key facts
>
> **Synonyms** are words with similar meanings: hot – boiling, roasting, scorching.
>
> **Antonyms** are words with opposite meanings: hot – cold, chilly, freezing.
>
> The best way to extend your **vocabulary** is to use a thesaurus.
>
> Look up any of the words below in a thesaurus and you'll find a list of synonyms.
>
> Many thesauruses also list opposites – antonyms.
>
> Deciding which **part of speech** you want will help you select the right kind of word.

Have a go!

1 List synonyms for these words:

a said: <u>remarked, stuttered</u> ....

b angry ....

c calm ....

d walked ....

e dirty ....

f jumped ....

g horrible ....

h wet ....

i cold ....

j eat ....

2 Now let's try antonyms. This time make a list of antonyms for each word.

For example:

bright: dark, murky, black, gloomy, overcast, ominous, dismal

a low ....

b pretty ....

c neatly ....

d shuffling ....

e quietly ....

Writing challenge 📄

Read this simple description of a visit to an island.

> ### Model text
>
> I arrived at the most beautiful island I had ever seen. The sea was shimmering in the sunlight as the palm trees fluttered in the warm breeze. I walked along the empty beach, listening to the gentle sound of the waves lapping on the shore. As I breathed in the perfumed air, I thought how lucky I was to find myself in such a wonderful place. It was a dream come true.

1 Write the 'synonym version' of this description, replacing the descriptive vocabulary with words of similar meanings to recreate the same scene.

2 Now try the 'antonym version' by changing the descriptive words to create an island scene that is quite the opposite!

sunny

rainy

Homophones

> ### Key facts
>
> **Homophones** are words that sound the same but are spelt differently because they have different meanings.
>
> For example:
>
> - It's there / (their) / they're table because there / their / (they're) sitting (there) / their / they're.
>
> - The queen is **rein** / **rain** / (reign)ing; in bad weather it's **rein** / (rain) / reigning; and I am (rein) / **rain** / **reigning** in the horse.
>
>
>
> Puzzling aren't they? And if you use the spellchecker on your computer, it won't help, because it can't detect a right spelling in a wrong context.

Have a go!

1 Circle the correct spelling – you may need to look some of them up in a dictionary to be sure.

   a My eye-site / sight helps me inspect the site / sight of the building.

   b The boy was delighted when he won / one more than won / one of the prizes.

   c I wonder who's / whose asking who's / whose bike this is.

2 Write one sentence that includes both homophones:

   a see / sea ....

   b no / know ....

   c blew / blue ....

   d read / red ....

3 Sometimes it's important to work out which word class you need. Write the words into the correct spaces in these sentences.

> For example: knew (verb – to know), new (adjective)
> I knew you would like the new book.

a licence (noun), license (verb)

The mayor will .... us to renew this ....

b ball (noun), bawl (verb)

The baby started to .... when he lost the ....

c write (verb), right (adjective)

I will .... the answer that is ....

d passed (verb), past (preposition)

I .... the bridge when I walked

.... the river.

e lead (noun), led (verb)

As she .... me down the path,

I noticed the .... on the roof.

f pale (adjective), pail (noun)

Jill grew very .... when she picked up the heavy

.... of water.

Writing challenge

Research and make a list of any homophones that have *three* spellings.

Are there any with four spellings? ....

Plurals

> ### Key facts
>
> There are four main rules for making 'regular' **plurals**:
>
> 1 For most words – just add *s*:   bug   bugs
>
> 2 For words ending in *ss*, *sh*, *ch* or *x* – add *es*:   box   boxes
>
> 3 For words ending in *y* – change the *y* to an *i* and add *es*:   fly   flies
>
>   but if there is a vowel before the *y* – just add *s*:   monkey   monkeys
>
> 4 For words ending in *f* or *fe* – usually change it to *ves*:   calf   calves
>
> Words that end with *o* usually add *es* in the plural – but there are some words that just add *s*.
>
> You often find that if a word ends in a **consonant** + *o* – add *es*, but if the word ends in a vowel + *o* – just add *s*.

Have a go!

1   Write the plural for each of these:

   a   one jelly, lots of ....

   b   one dish, lots of ....

   c   one loaf, lots of ....

   d   one plate, lots of ....

   e   one glass, lots of ....

   f   one cloth, lots of ....

   g   one table, lots of ....

   h   one shelf, lots of ....

   i   one coffee, lots of ....

   j   one cup, lots of ....

   k   one key, lots of ....

   l   one bench, lots of ....

2 Write the plurals of these words in the right tubs.

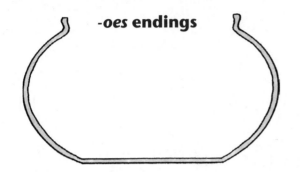

| tomato | piano | domino | radio | video | cargo | patio |
| disco | buffalo | photo | potato | mango | stereo | studio |

-oes endings

-os endings

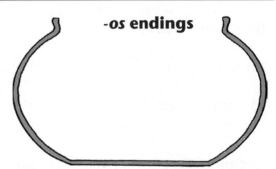

Writing challenge

Some words have irregular plurals.

Instead of simply adding *s*, they might change completely.
For example: man / men.

Other plurals stay exactly the same as the singular.
For example: deer / deer.

Make a list of at least 20 words with irregular plurals:

One (singular)	Lots of (plural)	One	Lots of
child	children		
sheep	sheep		
tooth			
foot			
ox			

How much can you remember? Test 4

1 Circle the correct spelling of each long vowel grapheme.

    (a) tayble / taible / table

    (b) creep / creap

    (c) pipe / pype

    (d) moan / mone   [4]

2 Underline the common letter patterns in these sets of words.

    (a) wedge   budge   ridge

    (b) hutch   stitch   catch   [2]

3 Write one new word for each of the letter patterns that you underlined above.

    (a) ....

    (b) ....   [2]

4 Write the correct word in each sentence.

    (a) The king ruled for fifty years. That is half a c.............................. .

    (b) The man was holding up a large p.........................of paper.

    (c) The boy was pleased to r.............................. his award.

    (d) In order to pass you need to w.............................. hard.   [4]

5 Complete each word with -*ant* or -*ent*.

    (a) extravag..............................

    (b) intellig..............................   [2]

6 Put four synonyms for the word **dark** in one box and four antonyms in the other.

> dismal   bright   dingy   brilliant   murky   gloomy   dazzling   light

synonyms	antonyms

[2]

7 Write a sentence for each of these homophones:

sail   sale

(a) ....

....

(b) ....

[2]

....

8 Write the plural of:

(a) a fly: ....

[2]

(b) a monkey: ....

Glossary

Adjective A word that comes before a noun to describe the noun.

Adverb A word added to the verb to give more detail about the action.

Alliteration A phrase containing a number of words beginning with the same phoneme.

Antonym A word that has the opposite meaning to another.

Apostrophe A punctuation mark (') that indicates possession or the omission of letters.

Audience The people who are going to read the text.

Autobiography A life story written by the subject of the story.

Biography A life story of a person written by someone else.

Character An individual in a story, poem or play.

Chronological Organised in terms of a sequence of events.

Clause A group of words that contains a subject and a verb.

Collective noun A group or collection of people, animals or things.

Comma A punctuation mark (,) that separates parts of a sentence.

Complex sentence A sentence made up of more than one clause.

Compound sentence A sentence made up of two or more clauses of equal weight, joined by simple connectives.

Comprehension Understanding of a text.

Connective A word used to link clauses.

Consonants All letters in the alphabet except *a, e, i, o, u*.

Dialogue A conversation written for a book, play or film, often between two people.

Direct speech Written conversation using speech marks; exactly what is being said.

Discussion text A text that presents both sides of an argument.

Explanation text A text that explains how or why something happens.

Fable A short story that teaches a moral lesson.

Fiction Invented / not true.

Formal writing Appropriate style and vocabulary when the audience and purpose is of a formal rather than informal nature.

Genre Type of writing.

Grapheme The written form of the phoneme.

Homophone Words that have the same sound but are spelt differently.

Imperative A command / order.

Inflection A change to the end of a word, to indicate tense or number.

Instruction text A text that is written to help readers to do something.

Main clause A group of words that can stand alone as a sentence.

Metaphor Writing about something as if it really were something else.

Narrative A recount of events, often in chronological order.

Non-chronological Organised without time sequence.

Non-fiction Factual writing.

Noun The name of a person, a place or a thing.

Paragraph Group of sentences about the same topic; denotes a change of content, place, time, action, and so on.

Parts of speech Word classes, for example: nouns, verbs, adjectives, adverbs.

Passive verb Opposite of 'active verb' – the subject is on the receiving end of the action.

Persuasive text A text that aims to persuade the reader to a particular viewpoint.

Phoneme The smallest unit of sound that can be heard in a word.

Phrase A group of words that work together as a unit.

Plural More than one.

Prefix A letter pattern that is placed at the beginning of a word to alter the meaning.

Preposition Small words that indicate time, place, direction, such as: *to*, *at*, *on*.

Pronoun Words used instead of a proper noun or noun, such as: *he, she, it, they*.

Punctuation Symbols used in writing that affect meaning and signal how something should be read.

Recount text A text written to retell; information organised in chronological order.

Report text A non-chronological information text to describe or classify.

Reported speech Saying what someone else has already said, sometimes without using the exact words.

Root word A word to which prefixes and suffixes are added.

Sentence A group of words that make sense on their own; begins with a capital letter and ends with a full stop.

Sequential language Language used to sequence actions or events into chronological order.

Setting The place and time in which a narrative is set.

Simile Describing something by comparing one thing with another.

Suffix A letter pattern added onto the end of a word and affects the meaning.

Syllable Part of a word.

Synonym A word that has the same meaning as another.

Tense Indicates time in the verb; the main tenses are: past, present and future.

Verb A word that expresses an action, a happening, a process or a state.

Viewpoint Someone's personal opinions on a topic.

Vocabulary The words we use.

Vowels The letters *a, e, i, o, u*.

The Publishers would like to thank the following for permission to reproduce copyright material:

Acknowledgements
Terry Nation: text extract from *Rebecca's World* (Red Fox, n/e, 1986), p8; **Evelyn Coleman:** text extract from *To Be a Drum* (Albert Whitman & Company, 1998), © 1998 by Evelyn Coleman, p10; **Lauren Child:** author biography from the publisher's website, www.orchardbooks.co.uk, and text extract plus illustration from *Utterly Me, Clarence Bean* (Orchard Books, 2003), reproduced by permission of David Higham Associates, pp12 & 22; **Eve Merriam:** 'Simile: Willow and Ginkgo' from *A Sky Full of Poems* (Dell Publishing Co, Reissue edition, 1986), copyright © 1986 Eve Merrian. Used by permission of Marian Reiner, p16; **Janice Cunningham, Sharon Hayles, Gladys Morgan, Karen Morrison and Daphne Paizee:** text extract from *Hodder Comprehension Book Six* (Hodder Education, 2012), p20; **Royal Society for the Protection of Birds:** 'Explore nature with a magnifying glass', including artwork by Mike Spoor, from *Bird Life* (May–June, 2006), p28; **Janice Cunningham, Sharon Hayles, Gladys Morgan, Karen Morrison and Daphne Paizee:** text extract from *Hodder Comprehension Book Six* (Hodder Education, 2012), p34; **Lynne Cherry:** front cover from *The Great Kapok Tree: A Tale of the Amazon Rain Forest* (Voyager Books edition, 2000), copyright © 1990 by Lynne Cherry, pp36 & 37; **Janice Cunningham, Sharon Hayles, Gladys Morgan, Karen Morrison and Daphne Paizee:** text extract from *Hodder Comprehension Book Six* (Hodder Education, 2012), p37; **Roald Dahl:** text extract from *Matilda* (Jonathan Cape, 1988), text copyright © Roald Dahl Nominee Ltd, 1988, p73. Photograph p22 © Dominic Lipinski – WPA Pool / Getty Images.

Extracts adapted with permission of Louis Fidge and Brenda Stones.

Every effort has been made to trace all copyright holders, but if any have been inadvertently overlooked the Publishers will be pleased to make the necessary arrangements at the first opportunity.

Sample test questions and answers are the author's own.

Hachette Livre UK's policy is to use papers that are natural, renewable and recyclable products and made from wood grown in sustainable forests. The logging and manufacturing processes are expected to conform to the environmental regulations of the country of origin.

Orders: please contact Bookpoint Ltd, 130 Milton Park, Abingdon, Oxon OX14 4SB. Telephone: (44) 01235 827720. Fax: (44) 01235 400454. Lines are open 9.00–5.00, Monday to Saturday, with a 24-hour message answering service. Visit our website at www.hoddereducation.com.

© Stephanie Austwick 2013
First published in 2013 by
Hodder Education
Carmelite House
50 Victoria Embankment
London EC4Y 0DZ

Impression number   5
Year   2017

Cover illustration by Peter Lubach
Illustrations by Planman Technologies, Simon Dennett at SD Illustration, Arthur Pickering, Kelly Gray, Tinny Rosser, Vian Oelofsen and Johann Strauss
Typeset in ITC Stone Sans Medium 12.5/15.5 by Planman Technologies
Printed in Spain.

A catalogue record for this title is available from the British Library.

ISBN: 978 1444 178289